SHE'S GOT GAME

WOMEN IN TRACK AND FIELD

by Sheila Llanas

WWW.FOCUSREADERS.COM

Focus Readers is distributed by North Star Editions:
sales@northstareditions.com | 888-417-0195

Produced for Focus Readers by Red Line Editorial.

Photographs ©: Matt Dunham/AP Images, cover, 1; Edmund Sumner/VIEW Pictures/ Newscom, 4–5; David Eulitt/MCT/ABACAUSA.com/Newscom, 7; Stephane Kempinaire/ DPPI/Icon Sportswire, 9; Ng Han Guan/AP Images, 11; La Vie au grand air: revue illustrée de tous les sports/Musée Air France/Bibliothèque nationale de France, 12–13; Koncern Ilustrowany Kurier Codzienny - Archiwum Ilustracji/National Digital Archive, Poland, 15; AP Images, 17, 18–19; Doug Mills/AP Images, 21; Bob Tringali/SportsChrome/Newscom, 23; Rob Tringali SportsChrome/Newscom, 24–25; David J. Phillip/AP Images, 26; Gustavo Ortiz/ picture-alliance/dpa/AP Images, 29

Library of Congress Cataloging-in-Publication Data
Names: Llanas, Sheila Griffin, 1958- author.
Title: Women in track and field / by Sheila Llanas.
Description: Lake Elmo, MN : Focus Readers, 2020. | Series: She's got game | Includes index. | Audience: Grades 4-6
Identifiers: LCCN 2019026844 (print) | LCCN 2019026845 (ebook) | ISBN 9781644930656 (hardcover) | ISBN 9781644931448 (paperback) | ISBN 9781644933022 (pdf) | ISBN 9781644932230 (ebook)
Subjects: LCSH: Women track and field athletes--Biography--Juvenile literature. | Track and field--Juvenile literature.
Classification: LCC GV697. A1 L598 2020 (print) | LCC GV697. A1 (ebook) | DDC 796.42082092/2--dc23
LC record available at https://lccn.loc.gov/2019026844
LC ebook record available at https://lccn.loc.gov/2019026845

Printed in the United States of America
Mankato, MN
012020

ABOUT THE AUTHOR

Sheila Llanas writes books for young people. Her favorite topics are poetry, nature, cooking, animals, music, history, and sports—to name a few! She likes to read, write, paint, and take long walks with her husband and their dog.

TABLE OF CONTENTS

ONE MINUTE TO GOLD

On August 10, 2012, four US sprinters prepared to race the 4x100-meter women's relay. They faced seven other teams inside London Olympic Stadium. The Jamaican team was the US team's biggest competition.

In a 4x100-meter relay, teams have four runners who each sprint 100 meters.

London Olympic Stadium held approximately 80,000 people during the 2012 Olympics.

To switch runners, teammates pass a baton, or small tube, between them. The US team had lost the last two Olympic races by fumbling or dropping the baton. They were determined not to make that mistake a third time.

The starting gun fired. Tianna Madison exploded from the starting block. She bolted around the track's first curve. She passed Jamaican gold medalist Shelly-Ann Fraser-Pryce. In a perfect exchange, Madison handed the baton to Allyson Felix.

Felix took the lead. Then she passed the baton to Bianca Knight. Knight flew down the track. She smoothly handed

Tianna Madison jumps off the block during the 4x100-meter relay at the 2012 Olympics.

off the baton to the **anchor**. Carmelita "The Jet" Jeter took off. In a blink, she crossed the finish line in triumph. The US women had won gold! They even set a world record for the 4x100-meter relay.

The record had been 41.37 seconds since 1985. The US team had finished the race in 40.82 seconds.

The US team wasn't the only team that did well. Jamaica and Ukraine won silver and bronze. These teams both set new national records as well.

PHOTO FINISH

In the 2016 Olympics, Allyson Felix ran the individual 400-meter race. At the finish line, she raced side by side with Bahamas star Shaunae Miller. Felix kept sprinting, but Miller decided to dive. She threw her body into the air and won gold by 0.07 seconds. Diving is not against the rules. The race ends when the athlete's chest crosses the finish line, not her feet.

The US women's relay team celebrates their world record time at the 2012 Olympics.

In the late 1800s and early 1900s, men had declared women too weak to compete in track and field. Since then, countless female athletes have proved them wrong. The history of women's track and field is filled with world-class stars.

ALLYSON FELIX

Allyson Felix's Olympic career took off when she was only 18 years old. In 2004, Felix won the silver medal in the 200-meter race. Four years later, she won gold for the 4x400-meter relay. But she got silver again in the 200 meters.

Longing for the 200-meter gold, Felix trained five hours a day. She did drills, sprints, and weight-lifting. On August 8, 2012, her hard work paid off. She won the Olympic 200-meter race. Her time, 21.88 seconds, nearly broke the world record. It was her first gold medal in a solo event.

After the 2016 Olympics, Felix's career total was six gold and three silver medals. She was the first female track and field athlete to win six gold medals. And she showed no sign of stopping.

Allyson Felix sprints during a 400-meter race in 2015.

CHAPTER 2

EARLY YEARS

The first modern Olympic Games took place in Athens, Greece, in 1896. Only men were allowed to take part. Four years later, 22 women entered the Olympics in Paris, France. However, these women only played sports that men said were "ladylike." These sports included croquet and tennis.

Hélène Prévost of France plays tennis during the 1900 Olympics.

Slowly, the Olympics added track and field events for women. By 1928, approximately 10 percent of Olympic athletes were women. That year, women competed in three races. Women also took part in the high jump and the discus. Halina Konopacka won the discus throw for Poland. She became the first woman to win a track and field gold medal.

In 1932, Mildred "Babe" Didrikson won two gold medals for Team USA. She won in the 80-meter hurdles and the javelin throw. She also took silver in the high jump.

In the 1950s, another US athlete overcame big odds. As a child, Wilma

In 1928, Halina Konopacka threw a world record distance of 39.62 meters (130 ft) to win the gold medal in discus.

Rudolph had polio. This illness can cause paralysis. Doctors said she might never walk. But she survived the illness. Then she began to sprint. A coach at Tennessee State University noticed Rudolph. He asked her to join the Tigerbelles. That track team was famous for speed.

Rudolph made it to the 1956 Olympics. She was only 16 years old. She won a bronze medal with the US women's 4x100-meter relay team. At the 1960 Olympics, Rudolph set records in

CIVIL RIGHTS CHAMPION

As an all-black team, the Tigerbelles faced a lot of racism. They were banned from using restrooms at some track meets. Some bus drivers refused to transport them. After the 1960 Olympics, Wilma Rudolph was a star. Her hometown of Clarksville, Tennessee, wanted to honor her. But the state's governor supported racial **segregation**. Rudolph said she would not attend a segregated event. As a result, Rudolph's parade and feast were the first desegregated events ever held in Clarksville.

Wilma Rudolph shows off her 100-meter gold medal from the 1960 Olympics.

the 100, 200, and 4x100-meter races. She was the first woman to win three gold medals in one Olympics. Fans called her the Black Gazelle and the Tennessee Tornado. Fans also called her the fastest woman in the world.

CHAPTER 3

TRACK AND FIELD CHAMPIONS

Athletes such as Wilma Rudolph inspired many girls to try track and field. Then Title IX passed in 1972. This law provided US women with even better opportunities. Title IX required colleges to spend a **proportional** amount of money on female athletes and male athletes.

In the 1960s, Kathrine Switzer joined Lynchburg College's only track team, which was all-male.

After Title IX became law, many young women flocked to college track teams. One of these women was Jackie Joyner-Kersee. Racing had not been easy for her as a child. But she'd stuck with the sport. One day, Joyner-Kersee tried the long jump just for fun. She had found what would become her best event.

Because of Title IX, Joyner-Kersee received a sports **scholarship** in 1980. She went to the University of California, Los Angeles (UCLA). There, Joyner-Kersee trained for the **heptathlon**. Between 1984 and 1996, she competed in four Olympic Games. She earned six medals, including three gold medals. In 1999,

Jackie Joyner-Kersee's best long jump distance was 7.49 meters (24.6 ft).

Sports Illustrated named her the Greatest Female Athlete of the 1900s.

The 1984 Olympics added new women's track and field events. Joan Benoit won gold for Team USA in the first women's **marathon**. Nawal El Moutawakel won the first women's 400-meter hurdles.

Her win gave Morocco its first gold medal. El Moutawakel was also the first woman from a Muslim-majority country to win gold in any event.

In 1988, Florence Griffith Joyner also became an Olympic star. She had been one of Joyner-Kersee's UCLA teammates.

ULTRAMARATHONS

Amy Palmiero-Winters had been a serious runner since childhood. In 1994, she lost her left leg below the knee. She needed a **prosthetic** leg. But Palmiero-Winters decided to keep running. In 2009, she began training for races longer than 100 miles (161 km). In 2011, she was the first amputee runner to finish the Badwater Ultramarathon. The race is 135 miles (217 km) through desert and mountains.

Florence Griffith Joyner sprints during the 1988 Olympics in Seoul, South Korea.

Griffith Joyner won three gold medals. She also set world records for the 100-meter and 200-meter races. As of 2018, her times were still the world's fastest. Athletes like Joyner-Kersee and Griffith Joyner brought new energy to the sport. Soon, new women trained to shine in track and field.

CHAPTER 4

THE TOP OF THEIR GAME

Many female sprinters made history on the track. Other women have soared in the field. These events include discus, javelin, and shot put. They also include pole vault and the hammer throw.

In college, Stacy Dragila wanted to try the pole vault. A male athlete told her women were not strong enough.

Stacy Dragila vaults over the pole during the 2000 Olympics.

Kamila Skolimowska's best hammer throw distance was 76.83 meters (252 ft).

Dragila proved him wrong. During the 2000 Olympics, she won gold in the first women's pole vault. She cleared 4.6 meters (15.1 ft).

Kamila Skolimowska won gold that year, too. The Polish athlete won the first women's hammer throw. She also became the youngest Olympic hammer thrower, male or female. She was 17 years old. Her gold medal throw traveled a total of 71.16 meters (233 ft).

THE JOURNEY OF SAMIA YUSUF OMAR

At the 2008 Olympics, Samia Yusuf Omar ran the 200-meter race. The Somali runner finished in last place. Even so, the crowd cheered her. Omar never had a coach or a real track to train on. A militant group controlled the city where she lived. The group banned women from sports. Omar wanted to compete again in the 2012 Olympics. But she had to leave Somalia to find a safe place to train. In April 2012, she boarded a **refugee** boat headed to Italy. Tragically, Omar drowned on the way.

Valerie Adams is another top athlete in field events. Adams is from New Zealand. In 2008, she won the gold medal for women's shot put. She also won gold in 2012. Between 2006 and 2014, Adams won a record-setting 107 shot put events in a row.

At the 2016 Olympics, a record 45 percent of athletes were women. This trend continues to encourage new girls. In the United States, nearly 500,000 high school girls take part in track and field every year. At the 2018 Youth Olympic Games, approximately 4,000 athletes competed. There were an equal number of girls and boys.

Hurdlers compete at the 2018 Youth Olympic Games.

Women's track and field has grown thanks to past athletes. These women jumped the highest, leapt the farthest, and ran the fastest. And they continue to inspire future generations of young women to follow in their footsteps.

FOCUS ON
WOMEN IN TRACK AND FIELD

Write your answers on a separate piece of paper.

1. Write a paragraph that describes the key ideas from Chapter 2.

2. Which track and field event would you like to do? Why?

3. Wilma Rudolph became the first woman to do what?
   A. win a gold medal in track and field
   B. win three gold medals in one Olympics
   C. win six gold medals in track and field

4. In a relay race, what makes passing the baton a challenge?
   A. The baton is heavy.
   B. Both athletes are sprinting.
   C. Other teams try to knock it away.

Answer key on page 32.

GLOSSARY

anchor
An athlete who runs the last leg of a relay race.

heptathlon
A track and field event that combines seven events, including the 100-meter hurdles, high jump, shot put, 200-meter dash, long jump, javelin throw, and 800-meter run.

marathon
A long-distance running race of 26.2 miles (42.2 km).

proportional
Having numbers or amounts that have the same relationship between one another.

prosthetic
Having to do with artificial body parts.

refugee
A person forced to leave his or her country due to war or other dangers.

scholarship
Money given to a student to pay for education expenses.

segregation
The separation of groups of people based on race or other factors.

TO LEARN MORE

BOOKS

Morganelli, Adrianna. *Wilma Rudolph: Track and Field Champion*. New York: Crabtree Publishing Company, 2017.

Rule, Heather. *Women in the Olympics*. Minneapolis: Abdo Publishing, 2018.

Stone, Ken. *Make Me the Best at Track and Field*. Minneapolis: Abdo Publishing, 2017.

NOTE TO EDUCATORS

Visit **www.focusreaders.com** to find lesson plans, activities, links, and other resources related to this title.

INDEX

Answer Key: 1. Answers will vary; **2.** Answers will vary; **3.** B; **4.** B